DATE DUE

15.95

977.5
Tho

Thompson, Kathleen.

Wisconsin

STECK-VAUGHN
PORTRAIT OF AMERICA

Wisconsin

Steck-Vaughn Company
Executive Editor Diane Sharpe
Senior Editor Martin S. Saiewitz
Design Manager Pamela Heaney
Photo Editor Margie Foster

Proof Positive/Farrowlyne Associates, Inc.
Program Editorial, Revision Development, Design, and Production

Consultant: Julia Hertel, Public Relations Manager, Wisconsin Division of Tourism

Published by Raintree Steck-Vaughn Publishers, an imprint of Steck-Vaughn Company.

A Turner Educational Services, Inc. book. Based on the Portrait of America television series by R. E. (Ted) Turner.

Cover Photo: Dairy farm by © Grant Heilman/Grant Heilman Photography.

Library of Congress Cataloging-in-Publication Data

Thompson, Kathleen.
    Wisconsin / Kathleen Thompson.
        p.   cm. — (Portrait of America)
    "Based on the Portrait of America television series" — T.p. verso.
    "A Turner book."
    Includes index.
    ISBN 0-8114-7396-1 (library binding). — ISBN 0-8114-7477-1 (softcover)
    1. Wisconsin—Juvenile literature. [1. Wisconsin.] I. Title. II. Series:
Thompson, Kathleen. Portrait of America.
F581.3.T46 1996
977.5—dc20   95-25728
                                                   CIP
                                                   AC

Acknowledgments
The publishers wish to thank the following for permission to reproduce photographs:
P. 7 Associated Milk Producers, Inc.; p. 8 National Museum of American Art, Smithsonian Institution, Gift of Mrs. Joseph Harrison, Jr.; p. 10 Wisconsin Department of Natural Resources; p. 11 State Historical Society of Wisconsin, Iconographic Collections; p. 12 State Historical Society of Wisconsin; p. 13 © Marion Ott Messner; p. 14 (top) © Doug Lyke/Ripon Commonwealth Press, (bottom) State Historical Society of Wisconsin; p. 15 (both), p. 16 State Historical Society of Wisconsin; p. 18 Wisconsin Maritime Museum; p. 19 The Bettmann Archive; pp. 20, 21 National Park Service; p. 22 Architect of the Capitol; p. 23 Wisconsin Department of Natural Resources; p. 24 Associated Milk Producers, Inc.; p. 26 (top) © Focus On Sports, (bottom) Wisconsin Milk Marketing Board; p. 27 (top) Wisconsin Milk Marketing Board, (bottom) Oscar Mayer Foods Corporation; p. 28 Miller Brewing Company; p. 29 Wisconsin Division of Tourism; pp. 30, 31 Wisconsin Milk Marketing Board; p. 32 Wisconsin Department of Natural Resources; p. 34 (both) SC Johnson Wax; p. 35 (top) © Cathlyn Melloan/Tony Stone Images, (bottom) UPI/Bettmann; p. 36 (both) Greater Madison Convention & Visitors Bureau; p. 37 (top) © Jim Morrill/The Great Circus Parade, (middle) Milwaukee Department of City Development, (bottom) The Bettmann Archive; pp. 38, 39 © Ginny Peifer; p. 40 University of Wisconsin, Madison Archives; p. 41 (top) University of Wisconsin, Madison Archives, (bottom) Wisconsin Department of Natural Resources; p. 42 © James Blank/Tony Stone Images; p. 44 © Doris DeWitt/Tony Stone Images; p. 46 One Mile Up; p. 47 (left) One Mile Up, (center, right) Wisconsin Department of Development, Division of Tourism.

STECK-VAUGHN

PORTRAIT OF AMERICA

Wisconsin

Kathleen Thompson

A Turner Book

RSVP

RAINTREE
STECK-VAUGHN
PUBLISHERS

The Steck-Vaughn Company

Austin, Texas

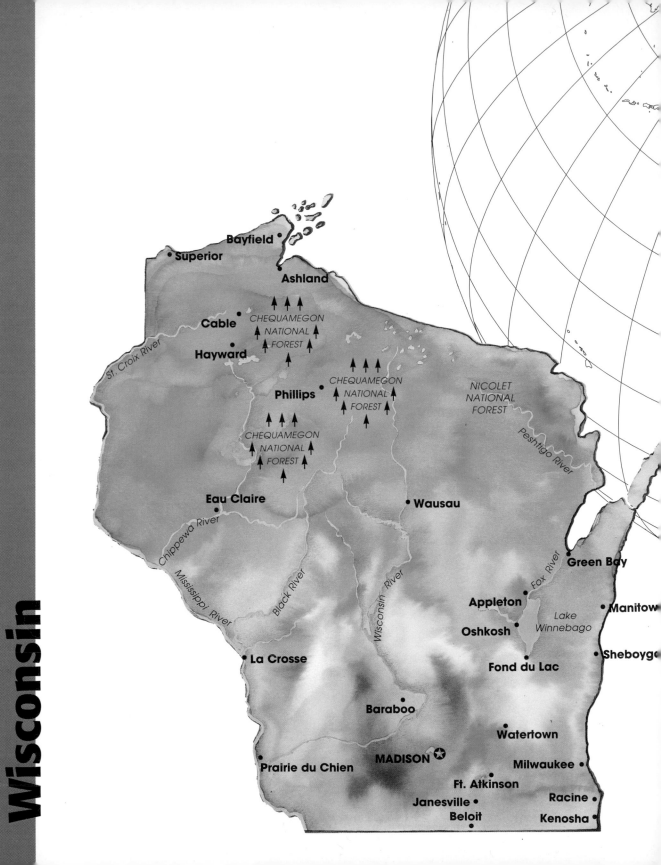

Wisconsin

Bayfield

Superior

Ashland

Cable

CHEQUAMEGON NATIONAL FOREST

Hayward

St. Croix River

Phillips

CHEQUAMEGON NATIONAL FOREST

CHEQUAMEGON NATIONAL FOREST

NICOLET NATIONAL FOREST

Peshtigo River

Eau Claire

Wausau

Chippewa River

Black River

Mississippi River

Wisconsin River

Fox River

Green Bay

Appleton

Manitow

Oshkosh

Lake Winnebago

La Crosse

Fond du Lac

Sheboyg

Baraboo

Watertown

MADISON ✪

Milwaukee

Prairie du Chien

Ft. Atkinson

Janesville

Racine

Beloit

Kenosha

Contents

Introduction

Wisconsin is America's dairyland. Just as dairy products make a body physically strong, dairy production has made Wisconsin economically strong. But Wisconsin is also famous for a certain kind of political leadership. Its progressive thinking has led to improvements in government that will last well into its future. The state has laws that help people and laws that preserve the environment. Perhaps Wisconsin is not quite as famous for its progressive thinkers as it is for its dairy products. But the laws that protect Wisconsin's future are as important to its people as dairy products are to their present.

There are 82,000 farms in Wisconsin. Most of them are dairy farms.

Wisconsin

Shaped by Glaciers, Made by People

About ten thousand years ago, the glaciers of the Ice Age began to melt, uncovering the area of Wisconsin for the first time in centuries. After that, ancient peoples migrated into the region. In the south-central region, there is a 172-acre village with a number of pyramid-shaped mounds. This village may have been built by the Middle Mississippians about one thousand years ago.

There are about 1,200 mounds in Wisconsin. They were constructed between 300 B.C. and A.D. 1000. A group called the Hopewells built some of them. Some mounds are shaped like simple hills. Others are shaped like living things—turtles, lizards, wildcats, and even people. Some of these mounds were used as burial sites, and other mounds were used for religious ceremonies.

By the time the Europeans arrived, several Native American groups—the Winnebago, the Chippewa, the Menominee, and the Potawatomi—had lived in the Wisconsin region for as long as a thousand years. Some Wisconsin Native Americans lived in wood lodges.

This portrait of Black Hawk was painted by George Catlin in 1832. In that year, Black Hawk defied the federal government by bringing his people back to the fertile lands of their ancestors.

9

The mounds at Aztalan State Park are all that remain of a four-hundred-year-old Aztalan settlement.

Others lived in wigwams made of curved branches covered with birch bark. These people lived by hunting deer and moose and gathering wild rice, berries, and nuts. Some grew corn and squash. They caught sturgeon, muskellunge, and other fish. Native Americans in the Wisconsin region traveled in canoes—some large enough to hold between 10 and 15 people. The glaciers left behind thousands of lakes and rivers, which made perfect "roads."

European explorers first arrived in the area in 1634. Jean Nicolet of France traveled through Lake Huron to Lake Michigan and finally landed near present-day Green Bay. Nicolet claimed the Wisconsin region for France and then returned to Montreal. Europeans didn't return to the area for about 25 years. Then French fur traders Pierre Esprit Radisson and Médard Chouart arrived. In 1661 Father René Ménard came to set up Catholic missions. In 1669 Father Jacques Claude Jean Allouez founded Wisconsin's first village, called La Bayne, in the place we now call Green Bay.

In 1673 Father Jacques Marquette and Louis Jolliet came to Wisconsin. They explored the Fox River, then carried their canoes to the Wisconsin River. Marquette and Jolliet followed the Wisconsin River to the Mississippi River, which forms the western edge of the state. They had found a great "road" for French exploration.

When Jean Nicolet landed in Wisconsin, he was sure he had found China. He put on a Chinese robe that he had brought with him, fired off his guns, and greeted the people on shore.

The French had good relations with Native Americans at first. But this eventually changed for two reasons. First, there was an increase in competition between the French and the Native Americans for land and other resources. Further east, the Iroquois were pushing Native American groups out of the Ohio and the Indiana regions. Some groups, such as the Fox, the Sauk, the Huron, the Miami, and the Illinois, moved west into the Wisconsin region.

Second, in 1712 the French decided to take control of the Fox and Wisconsin rivers because they were important trade routes. For 28 years the Fox and the Sauk fought the French for control of the rivers. The French finally won, but they lost their friendly relations with some of the Wisconsin Native Americans. That meant that the French had lost important allies.

Both France and Great Britain wanted to control the fur trade in America. The British also wanted more land. In 1754 the French and Indian War broke out. The British won the war in 1763, so France had to give

Lead mines were not always this roomy. Sometimes the ceilings were so low that miners worked on their stomachs.

up its claims to most of the land east of the Mississippi River. Even before the end of the war, many Native Americans left Wisconsin. The Miami went to western Ohio. The Potawatomi settled around what is now Chicago. The Kickapoo followed explorer René-Robert Cavelier, Sieur de La Salle, to the St. Louis area.

However, the British had their hands full with their colonies on the East Coast. In 1776 those colonies rebelled against Great Britain. The result was the Revolutionary War. It was fought far away from Wisconsin, so there were no battles of that war in the region. When the colonists won, the Wisconsin region became part of the new United States. There wasn't much real change. Wisconsin was too far from the colonies for the new government to take over. Some settlements were established in the territory. Solomon Juneau started a trading post in the area that later became Milwaukee. Other villages were founded on Lake Winnebago—places like Sheboygan, Fond du Lac, Oshkosh, and Appleton.

The Americans and the British fought another war—the War of 1812. That war ended in 1814 with a victory for the Americans, who took over British forts on the Great Lakes. By 1816 Americans controlled the fur trade in the new territory.

Very few people settled in the area immediately after the war. Then, in 1822 lead was discovered in southwestern Wisconsin. This mineral was used in paint and in buckshot for guns. Prospectors rushed to Wisconsin from the Virginia and Kentucky regions to mine the valuable mineral.

Native Americans in the Wisconsin region became more frustrated as more people moved onto their land. In 1832 the federal government ordered the Native Americans in Illinois to leave their land and move across the Mississippi into Iowa. Black Hawk, the leader of the Sauk and the Fox, rebelled and led nearly one thousand of his people back across the river into Wisconsin. The final battle took place near Prairie du Chien. Less than 150 of Black Hawk's group survived.

In 1836 Wisconsin became an official territory of the United States. Most of Wisconsin's 12,000 inhabitants lived in the lead-mining region. In 1848 Native Americans signed treaties giving away more of their land. They did this in the hope that Americans would be satisfied with the land they had already taken. Eventually the major groups were removed to reservations in the northern part of the state. After Americans took over these Native American lands, people from New England and immigrants from Germany, Great Britain, and Scandinavia came to the new territory in large numbers.

Originally the Wisconsin region was almost completely covered with forests. American lumber companies cut down the trees and sold the land for farms. It only took about fifty years for those loggers to cut down almost all the

Cornish miners moved to Mineral Point with their families. Their neat cottages line a street called "Shake Rag Street," because women would call their husbands to lunch by shaking a rag out the window.

This is the schoolhouse in Ripon where the Republican party is said to have been founded in 1854.

The Wisconsin and Northern Railroad constructed a bridge over the Wolf River in 1907. That same year, railroads began using steel passenger cars instead of wooden ones.

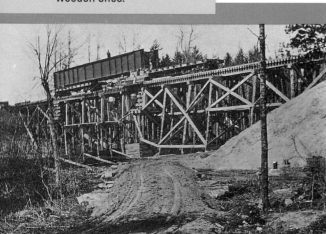

trees in Wisconsin. The farmers hauled away the tree stumps, plowed the land, and planted wheat.

In 1848 Wisconsin became a state. By 1850 there were more than three hundred thousand people living in Wisconsin. At that time, the biggest problem in the state was transportation. Ships traveled the Mississippi River and the Great Lakes, but it was hard to get crops from the farms to ports such as Milwaukee. The problem was solved in the 1850s when the railroad lines of the Northern Pacific Railroad came through Wisconsin. After that, Wisconsin farmers could ship their wheat to any market that had a shipping port or a railroad depot. Wisconsin became one of the most important wheat-growing states in the country.

The Civil War began in 1861. More than 85,000 Wisconsin soldiers fought for the Union. A group of Wisconsinites formed the Eagle Regiment, which had a bald eagle mascot named Old Abe. Perched on a special stand, Old Abe led the regiment into 42 battles and flew over the troops as they fought. Old Abe became famous all over the country. After the war, the state kept him in a place of honor in the state capitol.

Even before the Civil War ended, farming was changing in Wisconsin.

When Robert La Follette campaigned for President in 1924, he received almost five million votes.

The soil in the northern part of the state really wasn't good enough for growing wheat. Also, other states had richer soil and a better climate for that kind of agriculture. So William Hoard, a Fort Atkinson newspaper editor, talked to farmers about switching to dairy products. The farmers thought this was a very good idea. Soon people started calling Wisconsin the Dairy State.

From the time the Republican party began, Republicans had governed Wisconsin. Then, in the late 1890s, corruption caused a split in the party. Owners of the railroads were giving money to Republican legislators, who then passed laws that helped the railroads. But these laws hurt farmers. Some farmers even lost their land. A group of Republicans didn't like what was happening. In 1900 they ran Robert M. La Follette, Sr., for governor as a Progressive Republican, and he won.

"Fighting Bob" La Follette led the battle for social and economic reform. He had a theory called the "Wisconsin Idea." He believed that government should

People who contributed to La Follette's campaign received a "Progressive Bond" as a thank you. This was a bond of trust, not dollars!

MAY 30, 1904

MEMORIAL DAY
IN WISCONSIN SCHOOLS

THE MILWAUKEE [M] LITHO. COMPANY.

Old Abe led the Wisconsin Eagle Regiment into 42 battles. He was never wounded; however, he did lose a few feathers.

reach out to experts—a "brain trust"—to help it serve the people. La Follette's brain trust included experts in economics, politics, and administration. This trust helped Wisconsin adopt many new laws and procedures. One such law was designed to help workers who became injured on the job. Another provided a minimum wage for working women and children. In later years other states adopted these ideas.

In 1917 the United States joined the Allied forces against Germany in World War I. The war years were difficult for many Wisconsin citizens. Many had immigrated to the state from Germany and still had families living there. A number of Wisconsinites thought the German immigrants were traitors because Germany was the enemy in the war.

The war ended in 1918, but the tension didn't. For a long time, some people in the United States supported the temperance movement, which meant they were against drinking alcoholic beverages. The movement grew stronger during the war because many people associated beer with Germany, known worldwide for its breweries. Being against beer was a way for people to show that they were against Germany. In 1920, two thirds of the states approved the Eighteenth Amendment to the Constitution, which declared prohibition of alcohol a federal law. This amendment said that making, selling, or buying alcoholic beverages was illegal.

Prohibition was a problem for Wisconsin. Beer was important to the state's economy, and Prohibition put many people out of work. But after a while, it became clear that many Americans weren't obeying the law anyway. In 1932 Wisconsin was the second state to vote for the Twenty-first Amendment, which repealed, or canceled, Prohibition.

Wisconsin had other problems in the 1920s. Farms weren't making enough money. Lumber companies were closing because loggers had cut down almost all the trees. Then, in the 1930s, the Great Depression fell upon the entire country. Money was scarce and people couldn't find jobs. In 1934 drought hit the Midwest, including Wisconsin. Federal and state programs provided loans to farmers for seed and new equipment. The programs also helped farmers plant new trees and irrigate their land.

The devastating effects of Prohibition, the Depression, and the drought brought the Progressives back into power. In 1930 one of Bob La Follette's sons, Philip, was elected governor. In 1934 the Progressives became an independent party. Again, Wisconsin passed some of the most progressive labor laws in the country. The state had the first unemployment compensation law and programs to help farmers pay their debts.

One event solved the economic problems of the Great Depression—World War II. The United States entered the war in 1941, but even before that, Wisconsin industries were hard at work. The factories in the southeast produced tanks and army trucks instead of cars and farm equipment. Paper mills in the north made maps and books for soldiers. And people went to war. Wisconsin sent 375,000 soldiers to fight.

After World War II, the whole country saw a rise in manufacturing—Wisconsin, too. New farm machinery meant that fewer farm workers were needed. People moved to the cities looking for work in the factories. African Americans migrated from the South to cities such as Milwaukee. They were lured by more favorable laws toward African Americans and by the opportunity to make more money in the factories.

The dairy business suffered in the 1950s and 1960s. Lower milk prices combined with a change in the American diet to lower-calorie foods hurt the industry badly. In 1951 there were 132,000 dairy farms in Wisconsin. By 1969 there were fewer than half that many.

In the 1950s, Wisconsin senator Joseph R. McCarthy became known across the country for leading a crusade against Americans who had connections to the Communist party. For several years, Senator McCarthy falsely accused many people, from Hollywood actors to President Dwight D. Eisenhower, of being Communist "sympathizers."

A submarine is launched in Manitowoc during World War II. Manitowoc is a ship-building center and one of Wisconsin's largest ports.

Eventually McCarthy lost power, but not before he had damaged many people's lives and reputations.

In the 1960s and 1970s, many University of Wisconsin students protested against the war in Vietnam. In Washington, D.C., one of Wisconsin's more outspoken senators, William Proxmire, gave speeches against the war. After the war ended in 1973, Senator Proxmire turned his efforts toward ending wasteful government spending. Every month he announced his "Golden Fleece Award" to call attention to particularly wasteful government programs.

Democrat William Proxmire, who retired from the Senate in 1989, is well known for sponsoring the Truth in Lending Act, which protects consumers from hidden charges on loans.

In the early 1980s, Wisconsin—and the entire country—was hit by an economic recession. Many Wisconsin farm families sold their land and equipment. Also, many of the state's highly skilled workers lost their jobs when businesses left the state because of high taxes. In 1986 Wisconsin governor Tommy Thompson cut taxes to draw businesses to Wisconsin. Governor Thompson also initiated a state lottery and greyhound racetracks to bring in extra funds.

The 1990s in Wisconsin have seen many experimental programs designed to deal with the problems of the cities. Some of these programs are targeted for schools, welfare, and unemployment. Wisconsin's history of progressive, creative solutions to problems has not been left behind.

By the Shores of Gitchee Gumee

For hundreds, maybe thousands, of years the Chippewa have lived on the shores of the lake they call Gitchee Gumee. Today, its official name is Lake Superior. Gathering the fish of that lake provided the Chippewa with a living and was the basis of their way of life. They had a very special relationship with the land. The words of a Chippewa ceremony show their feeling: "From beginning to end it nourishes us: it quenches our thirst, it shelters us, and we follow the order of its seasons. . . . And when we die, we are buried within the land that outlives us all. We belong to the land by birth, by need, and by affection."

But that long history almost came to an end in the 1850s. All over the Midwest, Native Americans were being removed from their lands. The federal government was ordering one group after another to take their belongings to reservations located west of the Mississippi River.

The Chippewa of Wisconsin were one group that was supposed to leave. The government claimed that the Chippewa had signed treaties that gave the land to the United States. The Chippewa said they had never meant to lose their homes, they only meant to share the land. Those treaties said that the Native Americans retained their rights to hunt, gather, and fish on the land they had given up. Chief Buffalo, a Chippewa chief, knew that removal from their land would destroy his people. He knew that many would rather die than leave. So, at the age of eighty, he made the long journey to

The Chippewa of the Red Cliff Reservation have lived along the shore of Lake Superior for more than a thousand years.

The people of the Red Cliff Reservation own and operate the Buffalo Bay Fish Company. Fishing is a major economic activity.

Washington, D.C., to talk to President Millard Fillmore.

Henry Buffalo, the great-great grandson of Chief Buffalo, knows the story of that visit. Chief Buffalo told the government that he wanted reserved land that would follow the coast of Lake Superior all the way around to Sand River. The reservation would cover about 7,800 acres. At first, the Chief's arguments were ignored. But in 1851 the order for removal was suspended while everyone tried to work something out. In 1855 a new treaty was signed. The Chippewa could stay on the land that they called their home. For Chief Buffalo, that place became known as the Red Cliff Reservation. The land area is much smaller than what Chief Buffalo requested. It is on a tip of land that is farther north than any other place in Wisconsin.

More than one hundred years later, Wisconsin and some other Great Lakes states tried to take back the fishing rights that the old treaties promised to the Chippewa. The treaty stated clearly that the Chippewa were to follow the reservation's fishing regulations, not the regulations of any state. However, now the states insisted that the Chippewa follow the states' regulations. This time it was Henry Buffalo who fought back. He went to the Wisconsin Supreme Court with his law degree from the University of Wisconsin and a copy of his people's treaty with the government. In 1972 the court said that Henry Buffalo was right. The state couldn't tell the

This is a sculpture of Chief Buffalo.

Chippewa fishing fleet how, where, or when to fish. That was up to reservation law. The states were forced to accept the court ruling.

Today, two groups regulate commercial fishing boats on Lake Superior. Most commercial fishing boats are regulated by the United States government. Chippewa boats are regulated by Chippewa tribal law. In some places, this has caused tensions between competing fishing fleets. But near Bayfield, where Henry Buffalo lives, the two groups work together pretty well.

The Red Cliff fish hatchery has made relationships between the two groups a little easier. The hatchery began working in 1987. Its goal is to support the fishing industry. To do this, the Red Cliff hatchery raises lake trout, walleye, and whitefish from egg to "fingerlings" and "fry," which are early stages of a fish's growth. The young fish are released into the lakes and rivers when they are big enough to have a good chance of survival.

The goal of the Red Cliff hatchery is impressive. Every year, it tries to release 200,000 young walleye, 100,000 lake trout, and 500,000

Lighthouses have a long history on the Great Lakes.

young whitefish into the wild. This plan makes it clear that the Red Cliff fishing fleet will not endanger the supply of fish in the northern waters of Wisconsin.

There are still problems between Native Americans and the "newcomers" in Wisconsin. But one thing has changed. This time the Chippewa kept their home and their right to use it.

Building an Economy Through Variety

When people think of Wisconsin, they often think of cows in serene pastures. Americans have called Wisconsin the Dairy State for a long time. From 1920 to 1993, Wisconsin led the country in production of milk and other dairy products. Wisconsin has a diversified economy, however. That means that the state's economy relies on several different kinds of businesses. A diversified economy is good for a state because if one kind of business has problems, the others usually keep going. The whole state's economy doesn't suffer. Wisconsin has five major industries: dairy products, motor vehicles, paper products, meat products, and small engines. Tourism is a strong contributor to the state's economy as well. People visit Wisconsin in every season of the year.

Agriculture is important to Wisconsin. About 41 percent of Wisconsin's land is devoted to farms, mostly in the southern and central parts of the state. Farm products bring in $5.5 billion a year. About sixty percent of that money is from dairy products. But all

Most Wisconsin dairy farms have ample pastureland on which their dairy cattle graze. An average-size dairy farm maintains about 52 cows. Each cow produces about 1,600 gallons of milk every year.

25

Wisconsin farms aren't dairy farms. Wisconsin farms also raise cattle, hogs, poultry, and other livestock. In the southern region, there are many "cash crop" farms. Most cash crops are grown to be sold to markets or canneries. Door County is famous for its cherries. In various parts of the state, such as Monroe and Wood counties and the Lac Courte Orielles Reservation, people grow cranberries. Wisconsin leads the nation in the production of green beans, beets, cabbage, and sweet corn. Much of Wisconsin's cabbage is made into sauerkraut. Sauerkraut is so popular, there are even sauerkraut festivals in Wisconsin!

Even Wisconsin's farms are diversified. Marathon County, in the north-central section of the state, produces 95 percent of all the ginseng in the country—1.2 million pounds a year. Ginseng is a Chinese plant that is used for teas and other herbal preparations. The crop brings in customers from all over the world—even from China!

One thing that draws tourists to Wisconsin is the state's professional sports teams. Wisconsin is proud of the tradition of the Green Bay Packers, including the team's famous coach, Vincent Lombardi.

After the harvest some corn is left in the field until the kernels are dry. This corn is used as feed for cattle and hogs.

The state's northern reservations harvest tons of wild rice each year. And all of it is harvested by hand. Wild rice grows like tall grass in the shallow areas of northern lakes. The Chippewa of the Bad River Reservation paddle canoes out into the grasses, bend the individual plants over the bow of the canoe, and remove the rice by beating the seed heads with a stout stick. The rice is gathered in the bottom of the boat. This is their usual way to harvest wild rice.

Today, much cheese making is automated, but small specialty cheese shops produce their own brands and use traditional methods.

Food processing is part of Wisconsin's manufacturing economy. When food is processed, it is cooked or changed in some other way, packaged, and sent to market. Canned or frozen corn, for instance, is a processed food. So are cheese and butter. The town of Walworth is the home of Kikkoman Shoyu Co., Ltd., which turns Wisconsin soybeans into soy sauce. Medford is the home of Tombstone Pizza, a brand of frozen pizzas.

Oscar Mayer made Madison into a food-processing center by opening a meat-packing plant there in 1919.

Wisconsin's manufacturing, including food processing, brings in about eighty billion dollars a year and employs about 550,000 people. Most manufacturing is located in the southeastern and east-central sections of the state, including the Milwaukee area. Wisconsin leads the nation in manufacturing of small gasoline engines, power cranes, shovel hoists, mining machinery, and other kinds of industrial equipment. Wisconsinites make other things as well—farm equipment, electrical machinery, and paper products, for example.

It seems logical that Wisconsin makes paper products. Forests cover about forty percent of the state. Most are called second-growth trees because they were planted to replace Wisconsin's original forests. Some of the new forests are owned by paper or lumber companies. Wisconsin produces more paper than any other state, bringing in $12.4 million a year. Wisconsin companies such as Kimberly-Clark, which produces Kleenex and other well-known paper products, are known all over the world. Fort Howard Corporation is an international leader in using recycled wastepaper and wood to produce napkins and bathroom tissue.

Wisconsin's forests are also an important part of the state's tourism industry. Every year tourists bring about $5.5 billion to the state. Visitors hike through the forests and fish in Lake Michigan and the thousands of smaller glacier lakes. Tourists photograph the thousands of migrating birds that nest in Horicon

National Wildlife Refuge, a wetlands preserve that covers 31,000 acres in central Wisconsin.

But Wisconsin isn't just a place to visit in the summer. People come to ski and snowmobile in the winter, to wonder at the fall colors, and to participate in the year-round excitement of the casinos and the dog racetracks.

Restaurants, gas stations, motels, and hotels are all part of what is called the service economy. People in the service economy don't make products as people in a factory do. They do things for people, like cook their food or drive them to the airport. The service economy also includes financing and insurance. Milwaukee is a leading banking center in the Midwest and is the home of several major insurance companies. The service economy in Wisconsin employs about 25 percent of Wisconsin's workers.

So Wisconsin has a diverse economy. Its fishing fleet brings in more fresh fish than any other Great Lakes state. Wisconsin's Lake Michigan ports accept ocean-going cargo ships from all over the world. Janesville is the home of Parker Pens. Oshkosh B'gosh clothes are from Wisconsin, too. Practical items and healthy ways to have fun are the products of Wisconsin's economy. In more ways than one, Wisconsin provides America with what it needs.

Tourists can charter a boat and crew to take them out to the best fishing spots.

Down on the Farm

A hundred years ago, there were more cows in Wisconsin than there were people. But over the years, more and more people have moved from the farms to the cities. As a result, many people no longer know what it means to live and work on a farm. Those who haven't lived on a farm might not know that there's more to planting than popping seeds in a field and waiting for them to grow. Farm life is very demanding.

This is also true of a dairy farm. As Lisa Mullen puts it, "Running a farm is a seven-day-a-week, twenty-four-hour-a-day job. If you have a cow that's going to freshen [give birth to a calf] at one o'clock in the morning, you get up at one o'clock in the morning and you check on her. And if there's field work that has to be done before the weather gets bad, you've got to do that before anything else. Nothing can come before it."

Today, most dairy cows are milked by a milking machine. That may sound easy, but it isn't. Most dairy cows are milked twice a day, once early in the morning and once in the evening. Some are milked three times a day. The milking area has to be very sanitary to ensure that the milk will be safe. Barns have to be very clean, cows have to be

Dairy farming is hard work, and vacations are few and far between. After all, cows have to be milked every day.

Cows in a pasture are probably what many people imagine when they think of Wisconsin.

washed and prepared for milking, and all of the parts of the milking machine have to be sterile and handled with care. Everyone has to pitch in.

Dairy cows also need to be well fed, because a good diet ensures a healthy cow and high-quality milk. A cow's body gives milk in order to feed calves. People change that natural cycle so that the cow continues to give milk, even when there are no calves around. Milk production draws a lot of nutrients from the cow's body. A good diet is essential if the cow is going to stay healthy.

There are two ways to organize a dairy farm. Many farmers keep their cows in barns most of the time. The animals get their exercise by moving about in a relatively small area. Some

Wisconsin farms are not using this system. Instead they send their cows out to pasture, where they graze on grasses all day. Even so, the cows get additional special feed to maintain a healthy diet.

So, on a dairy farm, people need to milk, feed, clean, watch over, and care for the cows that produce the farm's product. Sometimes that means people have to be up early and have to stay up late. Why do dairy farmers do it? One farmer gave this explanation: "As far back as I can remember, way back in grade school, they told us we've got a hungry, hungry world to feed. And I think farmers . . . have tried to meet that challenge." That's a pretty good reason for working hard every day.

Wisconsin's Culture Is a Lifestyle

When you look at the culture of Wisconsin, you have to define what you mean by the word. For some people, the word *culture* means the fine arts—paintings, sculpture, classical music, literature, and theater. Wisconsin has all of these things. Milwaukee is the center of culture in the state. The Performing Arts Center is the home of the Milwaukee Symphony Orchestra, the Florentine Opera Company, and the Milwaukee Ballet Company. The Milwaukee Public Museum is famous for its exhibits of dinosaurs and the tropical rain forest.

Fine arts culture isn't represented only in Milwaukee, however. One of the greatest architects the United States ever produced is from Wisconsin. His name is Frank Lloyd Wright. Buildings that he designed are found all over the world. Taliesin, Wright's home for about fifty years, is located in Spring Green, in southwestern Wisconsin. Spring Green is also the location of an outdoor theater that produces plays by Shakespeare and other classical writers every

Breathtaking scenery such as this is the main reason why Wisconsinites enjoy an outdoor lifestyle.

This photograph shows Frank Lloyd Wright (on far right) at the construction site of the Johnson Wax buildings, which he designed.

summer. The American Players Theatre is nationally recognized for its work. In fact, in almost every Wisconsin town you'll find little theaters, orchestras, and bands.

Fine writers are also a part of Wisconsin's culture. Wisconsin is famous for writers such as Thornton Wilder, the author of two Pulitzer Prize-winning plays, *The Skin of Our Teeth* and *Our Town*. The Pulitzer is one of the country's highest honors given to a writer. Other Pulitzer Prize winners from Wisconsin are Hamlin Garland, Zona Gale, and Edna Ferber. These three authors wrote about frontier life in Wisconsin.

Culture might also be defined simply as "a way of life." In Wisconsin, not letting the cold winters and the hot summers bother you is part of the culture. Winter, no matter how cold or snowy, is a time for outdoor sports. There are 25,000 miles of snowmobile trails and 400 miles of cross-country ski trails. There are also 35 centers for downhill skiing and at least 15 parks where people can camp. Ice sailing is also a popular sport in Wisconsin. Boats are supported on either side with blades, like ice skates.

Frank Lloyd Wright designed the Johnson Wax building so that all workers would have plenty of natural light.

When the wind hits the sails—away you go! If you want to learn how to fish in the winter, just travel to Wisconsin. The biggest winter ice fishing event is the two-week-long season for catching sturgeon. Sturgeon average about one hundred pounds apiece!

Wisconsin's way of life is tied to the outdoors. The glaciers that once covered Wisconsin created about 15,000 lakes, hundreds of miles of rivers, and hundreds of miles of Lake Michigan shoreline. So Wisconsinites who prefer to sail on water instead of ice just wait for summer. The same is true for people who don't want to bundle up when they go fishing.

People who want to learn more about Wisconsin's special history can hike along a section of the Ice Age Trail. Hiking all of it would take a while—all in all, the trail is about one thousand miles long. This trail marks the edge of the glaciers that covered the area about ten thousand years ago. Two areas along the trail are especially important. One such place is Kettle Moraine State Forest. Moraines are gently rolling hills of soil that were left behind by the glaciers. Kettles are low places where rocks and other debris were deposited. Another place is Horicon National Wildlife Refuge, which is a wetlands and bird sanctuary in central Wisconsin. Glaciers had a profound effect on the way of life in Wisconsin.

Wisconsinites are very eager to celebrate their own and everyone else's heritage. Some people say that Milwaukee is the "City of Festivals," because the city sponsors one ethnic celebration after another. People dress in colorful costumes from the "old country," sell

above. The Mitchell Park Conservatory features controlled climates under huge glass domes. Rare plants and flowers grow there in desert, temperate, and tropical settings.

below. Harry Houdini, the famous escape artist, grew up in Appleton.

Milwaukee's Irish Festival celebrates Irish heritage. Many settlers from Ireland moved to Milwaukee in the 1840s.

Lake Monona in Madison is perfect for sailing, but people also fish, water-ski, and swim there.

ethnic food and handicrafts, dance, and sing traditional songs. French, Italian, Irish, Norwegian, German, African American, Mexican, Native American, Polish, and Greek festivals are enthusiastically attended. Milwaukee's ethnic festivals are the largest, but in every other major Wisconsin city, similar festivals take place.

Some cultural groups, such as the Menominee and the Oneida, have been in Wisconsin a very long time. Others have arrived more recently. Throughout many Wisconsin communities, there have been settlements of Laotian people called the Hmong. These hardworking people came to the United States from Laos after the Vietnam War. Their beautiful arts and handicrafts have greatly enriched the culture of the state.

Wisconsin has always been home to craftspeople and folk artists. For example, there's Fred Smith, a lumberjack from northern Wisconsin. Smith had no formal art training, but he did like making statues. He

used materials that were inexpensive or free, such as concrete, wood, and stone. For a while, everyone just thought his work was odd when they looked at his huge statues of farmers, kings, and cows. But today his works have been recognized and are displayed in Wisconsin Concrete Park in Phillips.

Wisconsin has a great deal of culture, ranging from traditional to modern. That's the way it is in Wisconsin. The people who live there honor every part of their lives.

Circuses are a tradition in Wisconsin, so every year Milwaukee holds the Great Milwaukee Circus Parade. During the rest of the year, the old circus wagons are stored at Baraboo in the Circus World Museum.

These three are enjoying the day at Milwaukee's Summerfest.

The Ringling Brothers Barnum and Bailey Circus had a small beginning. It started when five brothers liked a clown so much that they decided to start a circus of their own.

RINGLING BROS
AND BARNUM & BAILEY
COMBINED SHOWS

THE GREATEST SHOW ON EARTH

Norway's Olympic Cousin: The American Birkebeiner

Every February about six thousand people come to northern Wisconsin, just outside Hayward. They come to participate in an international cross-country skiing race. The 31-mile race is called the American Birkebeiner. The race is part of the cross-country ski competitions that qualify people for the Olympic Games. The American Birkebeiner is the largest cross-country skiing race in the United States.

The race is based on one that is held in Norway. And that race is based on a real event that took place in the early 1200s. At that time there was a civil war in Norway. An infant boy named Haakon Haakonson, who was heir to the throne, was in danger. So two loyal men, Torstein Skevla and Skjerval Skrukka, rescued the boy and carried him through the mountains to

Everyone in Hayward calls the Birkebeiner by its nickname, the "Birkie."

a safe place 31 miles away. They traveled by skiing the whole distance, since the snow was so deep. The name of the race—*Birkebeiner*—is the word for the birchbark leggings that those skiers wore. The event is repeated every year in Norway in a race that follows the same path that Skevla and Skrukka took. Racers don't carry an infant! Instead they carry a 12-pound pack.

The American Birkebeiner race follows a path from a resort called Telemark, just outside the town of Cable. The resort is named after a mountain in Norway. The race is a difficult one. Part of the difficulty is the length. The Birkebeiner's 31-mile-long trail runs over rough ground, up and down steep hills, and through forests. The highest section of the race is Mt. Telemark. It is almost 1,700 feet higher than the lowest section of the race.

The excitement is high on the day of the Birkebeiner. As one racer described it, "As you get to the starting line, it's much like a group of stallions. They stamp their skis and the music is blaring and it just builds and builds and builds until finally the

The first Birkebeiner was run in 1973 and had only 53 skiers.

cannon fires and . . . wow! They're all going."

The American Birkebeiner is a week-long celebration. Included are a short race that is half as long as the big race, ski-archery contests (which combine cross-country skiing and archery), a biathlon (which combines cross-country skiing and target shooting), and other events for anyone who loves winter sports.

Changing the World

Aldo Leopold is called the father of the environmental movement, which is dedicated to protecting our environment from the damage we do to it. Aldo Leopold loved the outdoors. He worked for the United States Forest Service for 15 years. He felt strongly that people should enjoy parks and forests. He also believed that people should leave the wilderness areas just the way they found them. And he wasn't shy about saying so.

Aldo Leopold's ideas got around. In 1933 the University of Wisconsin hired him to teach a brand-new area of study called wildlife management science. Aldo Leopold taught his new students his ideas about conserving and protecting natural areas. It was during this time that he came up with a truly great idea. He established the University of Wisconsin Arboretum, a place where trees and plants are grown for scientific or educational purposes. Many schools have arboretums now. But in the early 1930s, no one had ever heard of such a thing. The University of Wisconsin Arboretum

Aldo Leopold studied forestry at Yale University in the early 1900s.

is an outdoor museum of flowers, plants, and trees, covering 1,280 acres. One of the most interesting features of the arboretum is a section of restored prairie land called Curtis Prairie. This section of actual prairie land measures 2.5 square miles. Many of the prairie's plants and grasses were at one time very close to becoming extinct. But in the protected area of the arboretum they were allowed to grow in their natural environment. In fact, Curtis Prairie looks pretty much like the land the early American pioneers crossed many years ago. There are more than

This photo of Aldo Leopold was taken in 1947, a year before he died.

400 prairie plant species and 248 varieties of birds living in this area.

Aldo Leopold wrote books and articles about the need to treat the environment with care. His most famous book is *A Sand County Almanac*. It details his experiences working on his farm outside Baraboo, Wisconsin. The book, which was published in 1949 after his death, is considered a classic guide to the study of ecology and land use.

In 1948 Aldo Leopold died fighting a grass fire on a neighbor's farm. The land around his farm was later made into a nature preserve. It stands as a tribute to a person who worked all his life to protect the natural environment and to inspire others to do so, too.

The Kettle Moraine is typical of southern Wisconsin, where Aldo Leopold spent much of his life.

On, Wisconsin

Wisconsin joined the Union 72 years after the Declaration of Independence was signed. Although the state's population started with a boom, for the most part the population has grown steadily since. People think that the same steady pattern will continue.

That is good news for Wisconsin's future, but the state faces some tough issues, too. The southeastern corner of the state has all of the problems that concern other cities in the United States. Wisconsin has to find work for its unemployed, provide decent housing, and supply good schools and other city services.

But Wisconsin's most serious problem may be its environment, especially its water. In 1993 Milwaukee's drinking water became polluted with harmful bacteria. More than three hundred thousand people became ill, and some died. Some people think that the pollution was caused by agriculture. Rain fell on agricultural land and washed waste from cows and pigs into rivers. The rivers carried the contaminated water to Lake Michigan, which is a source of drinking water for

Milwaukee is Wisconsin's largest city and a transportation hub for the entire state.

Milwaukee and other cities. This problem has raised questions that clearly show the conflict between the environment and the economy. Wisconsinites have to find ways to provide safe drinking water without putting harmfully tight restrictions on farms.

Dairy farmers are also facing questions that affect everyone. Recently a company developed a substance called bovine growth hormone (BGH) that can make cows give more milk. The federal government has stated that BGH is not harmful to people who drink the milk. Some farmers disagree and argue that the country has enough milk as it is, so BGH is not necessary. However, some farmers may go out of business if they don't use it. They won't be able to compete with farms whose cows are producing more milk. What is the best thing to do?

There are no easy answers to these questions. It will take all of Wisconsin's traditional common sense to solve them. Maybe as Wisconsinites answer their questions they will pave the way for the rest of the country, just as they did in the days of "Fighting Bob" La Follette. That's not a bad tradition to follow.

New housing was built along the Milwaukee River to accommodate Milwaukee's rising population. One third of Wisconsinites live in Milwaukee.

Important Historical Events

1000 Present-day Native American groups begin to move into Wisconsin.

1634 French explorer Jean Nicolet lands at Green Bay.

1660 Fur traders Pierre Esprit Radisson and Médard Chouart explore the Lake Superior shore in search of furs.

1661 Father René Ménard is the first missionary to visit the area. He establishes a Roman Catholic mission, near Ashland.

1673 Louis Jolliet and Father Jacques Marquette pass through Wisconsin, exploring its waterways.

1712 War breaks out between the French and the Fox. Both want control of the Fox and Wisconsin rivers.

1740 The French defeat the Fox.

1787 Wisconsin becomes part of the Northwest Territory.

1800 Wisconsin is included in part of the Indiana Territory.

1809 Wisconsin forms part of the Illinois Territory.

1814 Americans take over the British forts in the Wisconsin region. Fort Shelby is built at Prairie du Chien.

1836 The Wisconsin Territory is created. Madison is the capital, and the governor is Henry Dodge.

1845 Swiss colonists in New Glarus make the first cheese in Wisconsin.

1848 Wisconsin joins the Union on May 29 as the 30th state. Native American lands are signed over to the state in a number of treaties.

1854 The Republican party movement begins in Ripon.

1856 The Republican party becomes a powerful force in Wisconsin as the state's first Republican governor, Coles Bashford, takes office. The first kindergarten in the United States opens at Watertown.

1871 A huge forest fire destroys Peshtigo and nearby villages, killing 1,200 people.

1872 The Wisconsin Dairymen's Association is organized at Watertown.

1900 Robert La Follette leads a progressive faction of the Republican party and wins the governorship.

1911 The state legislature passes many progressive reform laws.

1921 Women are given full civil and property rights in Wisconsin.

1924 La Follette is defeated by Republican Calvin Coolidge for the presidency of the United States.

1934 Drought destroys thousands of acres of Wisconsin farms.

1950 to 1954 Senator Joseph McCarthy holds hearings on suspected communists in the federal government.

1959 The St. Lawrence Seaway is finished, making seaports out of Wisconsin's Great Lakes cities.

1961 The Menominee are given freedom from federal control. Their reservation becomes the state's 72nd county.

1973 Senator William Proxmire begins his "Golden Fleece Awards."

1980 The first Native American casinos are built on Wisconsin reservations.

1993 Northern portions of the Mississippi River valley are flooded. President Bill Clinton declares parts of Wisconsin disaster areas.

In the center of the state flag is a gold shield divided into four quarters. In each quarter is a symbol of Wisconsin's economic life: plow, shovel and pick, anchor, and sledgehammer. Standing to the left of the shield is a navigator; to the right is a miner. Just above the shield is a badger. Above it is the state motto. Below the shield is the year that Wisconsin became a state.

WISCONSIN

1848

Wisconsin Almanac

Nickname. The Badger State

Capital. Madison

State Bird. Robin

State Flower. Wood violet

State Tree. Sugar maple

State Motto. Forward

State Song. "On, Wisconsin!"

State Abbreviations. Wis. (traditional); WI (postal)

Statehood. May 29, 1848, the 30th state

Government. Congress: U.S. senators, 2; U.S. representatives, 9. State Legislature: senators, 33; representatives, 99. Counties: 72

Area. 56,145 sq mi (145,414 sq km), 26th in size among the states

Greatest Distances. north/south, 314 mi (506 km); east/west, 293 mi (472 km)

Elevation. Highest: Timms Hill, 1,952 ft (595 m). Lowest: 581 ft (177 m)

Population. 1990 Census: 4,906,745 (4% increase over 1980). Density: 87 persons per sq mi (34 persons per sq km). Distribution: 66% urban, 34% rural. 1980 Census: 4,705,335

Economy. *Agriculture*: milk, beef cattle, hogs, corn. *Manufacturing*: machinery, food products, paper products, fabricated metal products, electrical equipment. *Mining*: crushed stone, sand and gravel, iron ore

State Seal

State Flower: Wood violet

State Bird: Robin

Annual Events

★ World Championship Snowmobile Derby in Eagle River (January)

★ Ski-jumping tournaments in Middleton and Westby (January/February)

★ Syttende Mai Norwegian Festival in Stoughton and Westby (May)

★ Summerfest in Milwaukee (June)

★ Lumberjack World Championship in Hayward (July)

★ Experimental Aircraft Association Fly-In in Oshkosh (July)

★ Wisconsin State Fair in West Allis (August)

★ World Dairy Exposition in Madison (October)

Places to Visit

★ Apostle Islands in Lake Superior, offshore from Bayfield

★ Cave of the Mounds, near Blue Mounds

★ Circus World Museum in Baraboo

★ Clown Hall of Fame in Delevan

★ Devil's Lake State Park (part of the Ice Age National Scientific Reserve), near Baraboo

★ Door County, on Door Peninsula

★ Fort Crawford Medical Museum in Prairie du Chien

★ House of the Rock, north of Dodgeville

★ Little Norway, near Mount Horeb

★ Old World Wisconsin, near Eagle

★ Taliesin, near Spring Green

Index